Spears were used to hunt animals. There were many types of spears. Fish spears were light.

Spear tips were made to be sharp. A spear tip could be made from stone. Spears could be made from bones.

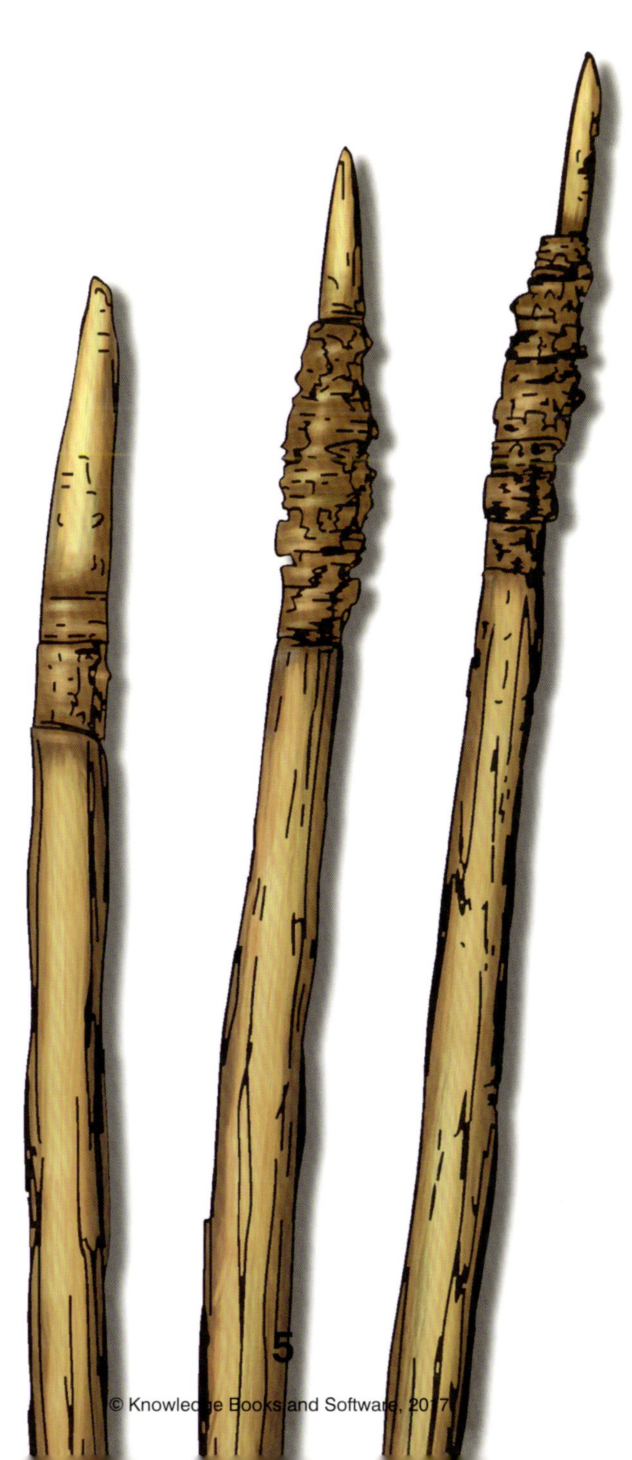

Stone spear tips were very sharp. These spears were used for hunting animals. The spear tip was made from flakes of stone.

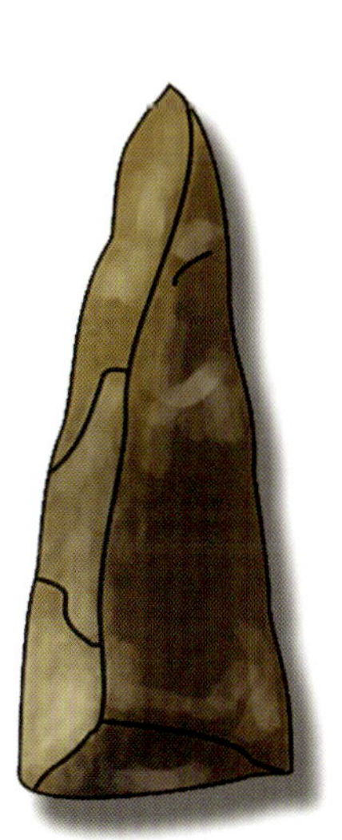
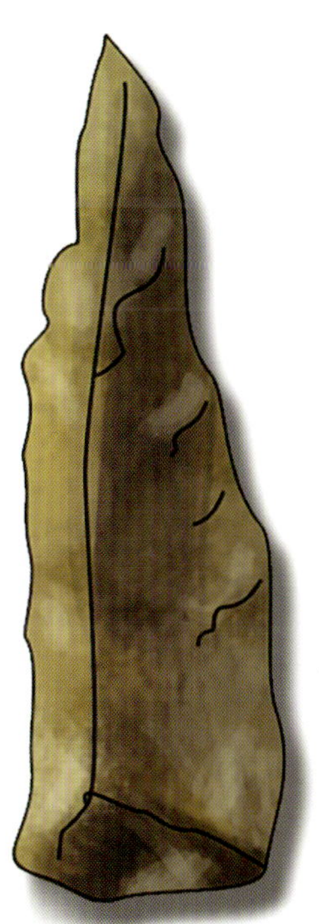
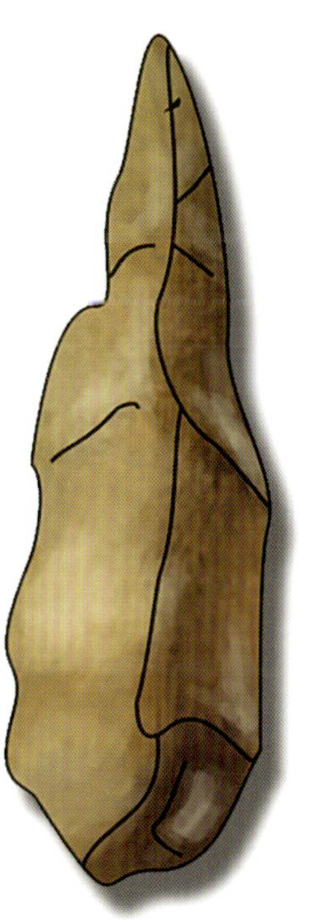

String was made from dry plants and hair. The spear tip was tied on using string.

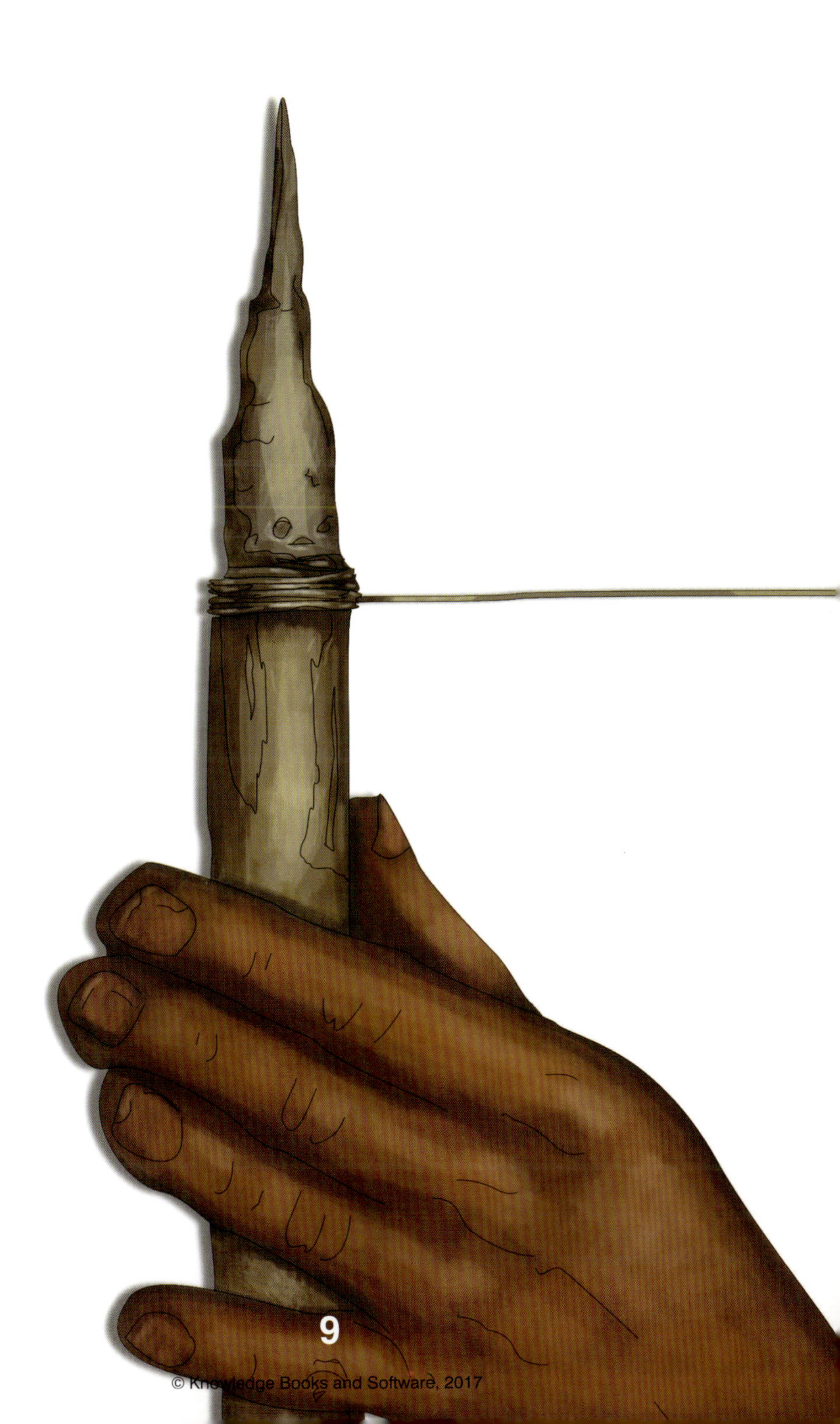

Gum from plants was put with the string. The gum was made soft by heating. The gum was hard and strong.

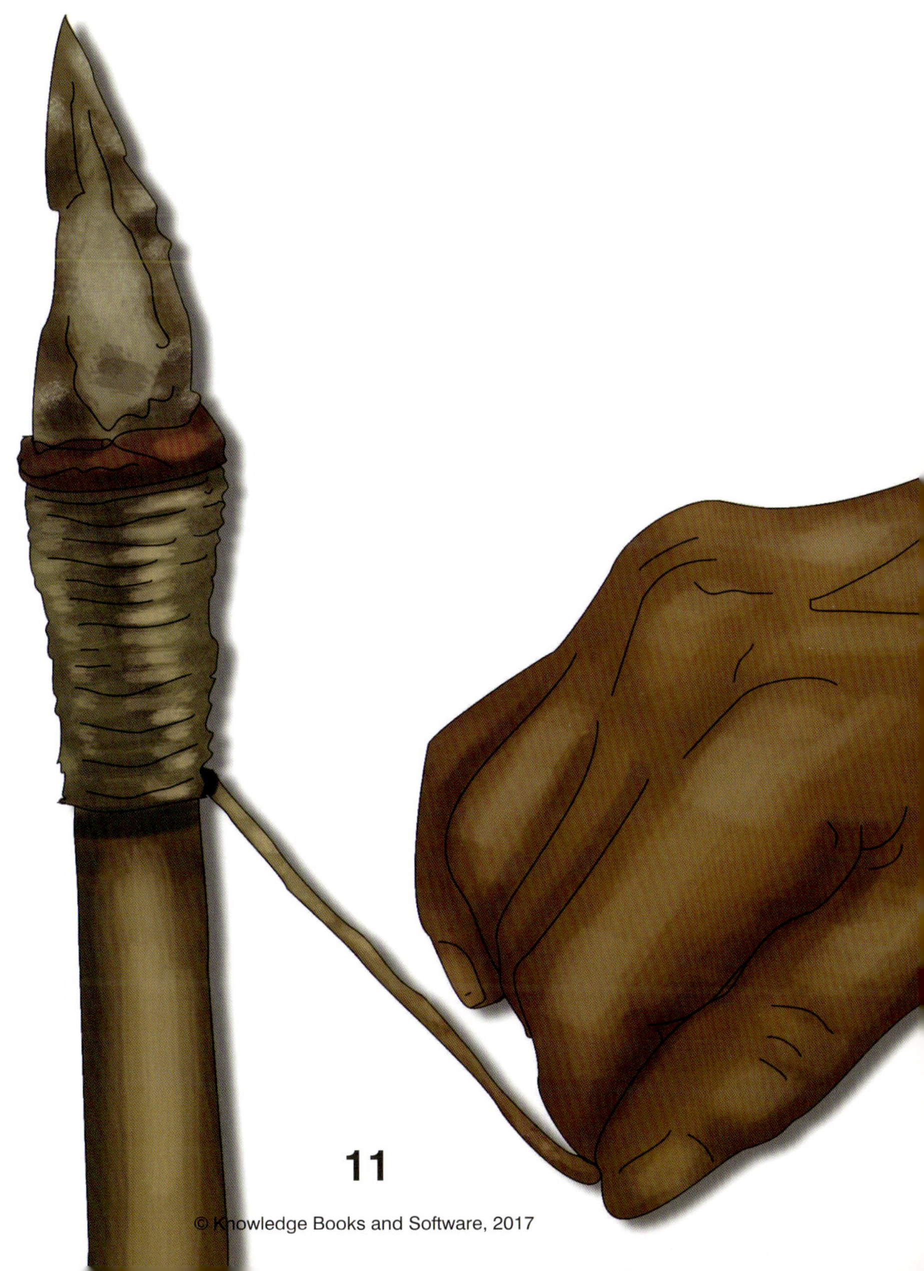

Spears had to be straight. Heat and bend the spear until straight.

Hunting spears had spear tips for the size of the animal. Spear tips for fish were lighter and could have two tips. Sometimes spear tips were like big fish hooks.

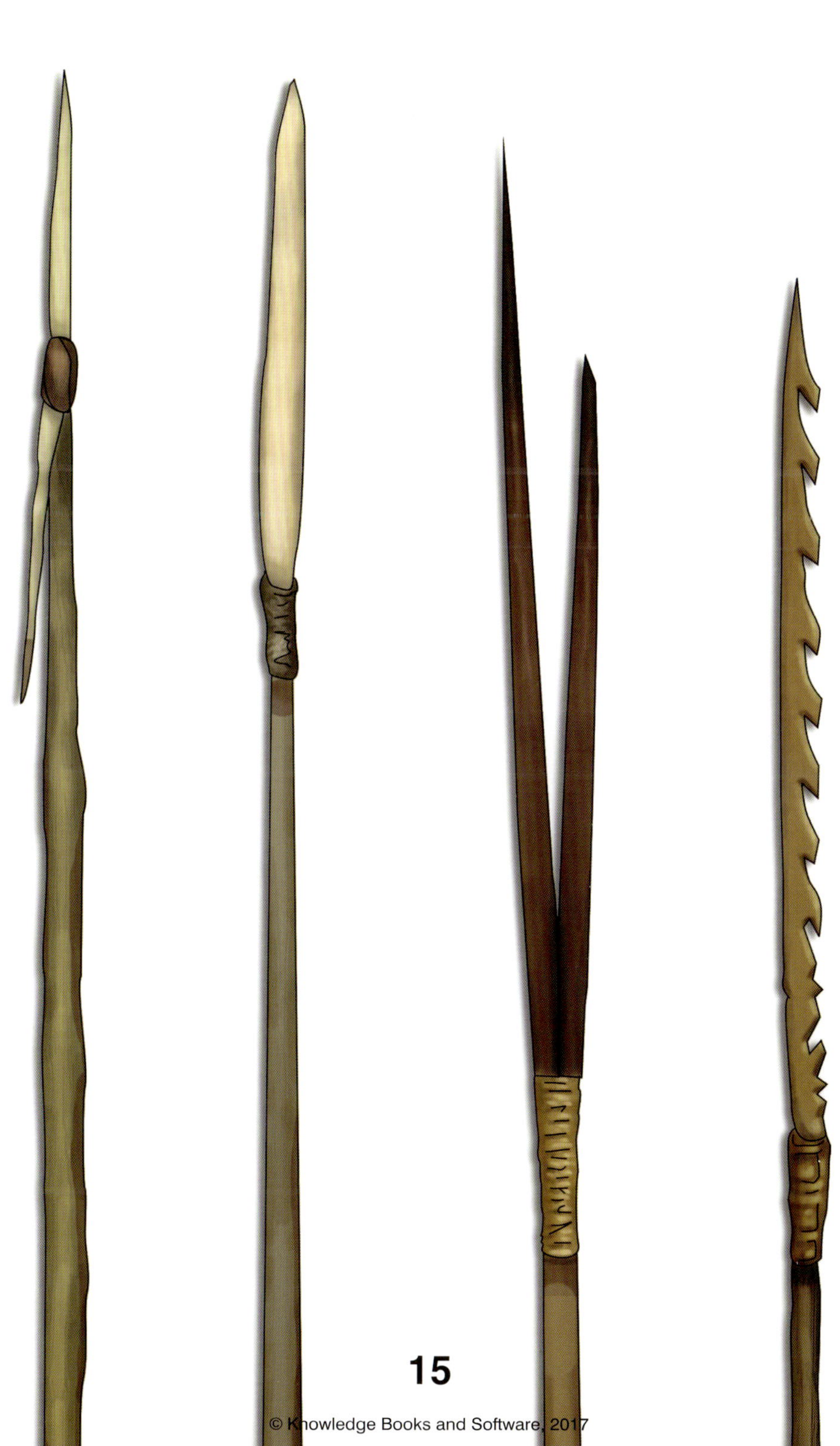

A long light spear was used for spearing fish. The fish spear had two tips. Fish were hunted from a canoe.

A spear has to be thrown quickly.
Long spears were hard to throw.

Spears were painted for many uses. The paint would come from plants and ochre.

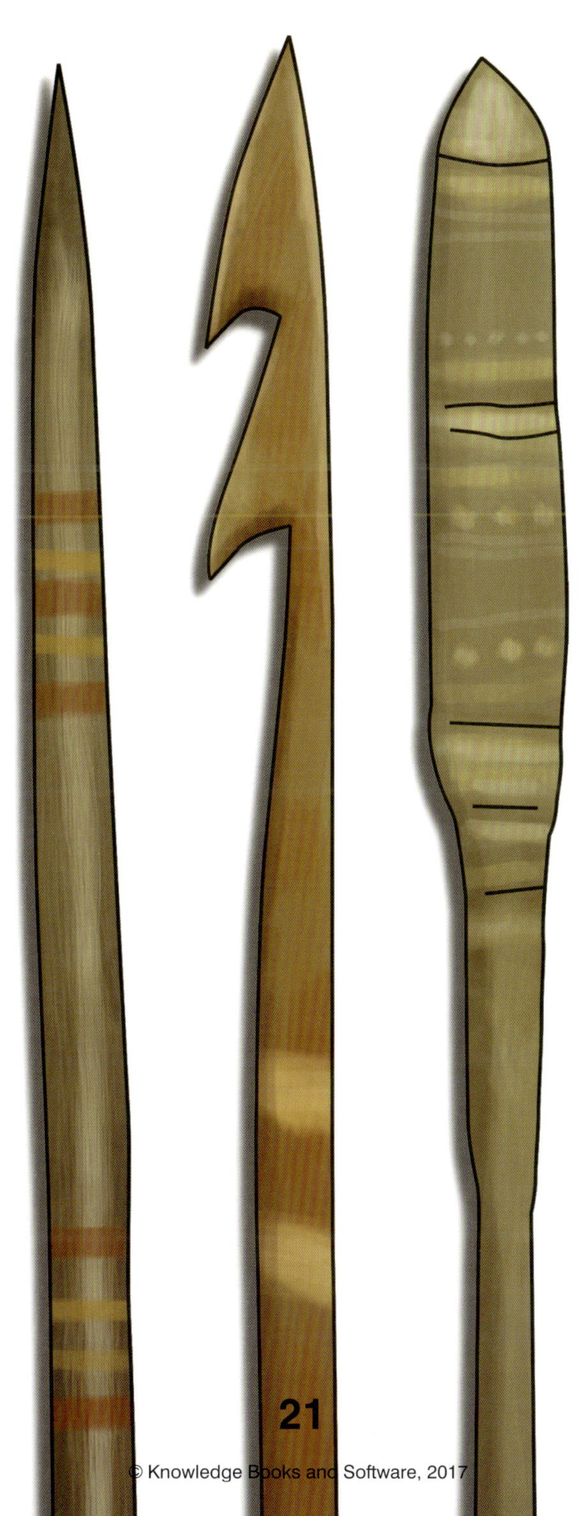

Spear tips could be made by hitting flakes to have sharp sides. The remains of these spear tips can be found across Australia. Leave the spear tips where you found these tools.

Word bank

spears

animals

Australia

flakes

string

gum

heating

strong

straight

bend

lighter

sometimes

quickly

ochre

sharp

remains